Tinderbox Lawn

Prose Poems by Carol Guess

Also by Carol Guess

Love Is A Map I Must Not Set On Fire
(VRZHU Press, 2008)

Femme's Dictionary
(Calyx Books, 2004)

Gaslight
(Odd Girls Press, 2001)

Switch
(Calyx Books, 1998)

Seeing Dell
(Cleis Press, 1996)

Advance Praise for *Tinderbox Lawn*

"*Tinderbox Lawn* will light you on fire. The music is broken glass; the buildings in flame. Even the language is bruised 'blue and purple.' Richly steeped in the violence of loss, these poems are a tea 'so sharp it cuts teacups to shards.' And one wants to keep drinking—for the war planes and train whistles, the queer girls in dresses, for Guess's vulnerable and unbreakable voice."

—Jen Currin, author of *The Sleep of Four Cities*

"The sharply cut lines of *Tinderbox Lawn* veer from the stark and crystalline [. . .] to the blur of memory and dreams [. . .] And between those conditions the possibility and impossibility of love lingers throughout, amidst vivid details of urban spectacle. Carol Guess, through brilliantly wrought blocks of prose, has made the kind of poetry you'll want to keep on your night-stand; poetry that won't leave the back of your head—the pulse and insistent whisper of it—a 'bridge between faith and decay.'"

—Joseph Massey, author of *Out of Light*

Tinderbox Lawn

·

Prose Poems by Carol Guess

Rose Metal Press

2008

Rose Metal Press, Inc.
P.O. Box 1956
Brookline, MA 02446
rosemetalpress@gmail.com
www.rosemetalpress.com

Library of Congress Control Number: 2008938198

ISBN: 978-0-9789848-5-4

Cover and interior design by Melissa Gruntkosky
Cover typefaces: Scala and Scala Sans
Interior typeface: Dante
See "A Note About the Type" for more information about the type.

Cover art: *Purple Plums* by Lorraine Peltz. Lorraine Peltz is an artist who
lives in Chicago and teaches at the School of the Art Institute of Chicago.
Her work is represented by Cheryl McGinnis Gallery, NYC; Micaela
Gallery, San Francisco; and Koscielak Gallery, Chicago. More info and
images can be viewed on her website: www.lorrainepeltz.com

This book is manufactured in the United States of America and printed
on acid-free paper.

Credit: The epigraph is from Richard Siken's poem "Scheherazade," pub-
lished in his book *Crush*. Used with permission of Yale University Press.

Acknowledgments

—————————•—————————

Thanks to *Bat City Review, Black Warrior Review, Hayden's Ferry Review, Knockout, Mid-American Review,* and *Poemeleon,* where portions of this collection first appeared in slightly different forms.

Thanks to my family and friends.

Special thanks to Abigail Beckel and Kathleen Rooney; to Lorraine Peltz; and to Tina Claussen, Amy Fanning, Jeremy Halinen, Mandy Laughtland, and Leigh Ann Morlock.

For Elizabeth J. Colen

Table Of Contents

Tell me how all this, and love too, will ruin us.
These, our bodies, possessed by light.
Tell me we'll never get used to it.

Richard Siken, "Scheherazade"

one

·

Walk All Ways
With Walk

You sell everything you own. Force the five fingers of your only hand into your palm, fist the stone you skipped as a girl. You were a boy then. The secret of skipping was never wanting a ring. Water was home, if only inside you. The places it took you required departures, skirt after skirt, dirt under the wheels of your truck. Stuck in a ditch past Lincoln you left that, too, shirt on your back sweet as the last girl's head thrown back, bed of your truck, sky as water, blue above both of you, her legs always opening, light changing green to Walk All Ways With Walk. You wade past the logjam into the sea. *Anna, Susanna, Matilda, Marie.* What comes next? No one knows—not the red-winged blackbird, not the preacher. You enter a solitude you will never escape. A million televisions blame someone else as your beautiful country erupts into Empire. You cover your ankles and your waist with water. *Aretha, Denira, Tamika, Louise.*

In Nebraska the sun is a terrible lion that will chase you down the road you live on. In Nebraska you must cover your mouth when you speak of God. In Nebraska work is always hard and the temperature consults with the leaves before falling. In Nebraska words cost more than bread. In Nebraska people still listen to records, bright stacks of vinyl for weddings and funerals. Tall grasses sway like water, glint more beautifully than any river. Nebraska doesn't give a shit about New York or L.A. Nebraska has corn, wheat, and cattle. Nebraska has cakes slathered in icing so thick bakers drown at birthdays. Nebraska has an annual March for Jesus and a March for Cheeses that is not the same thing. You have learned many Nebraska lessons. You know how to cover your nose with a cloth to snuff out the smell of the stockyards. You know how to bow your head before dinner, how to close the curtains before you have sex. You know how not to get killed in Nebraska. How to drive in whiteout as if parting the sea.

When you first begin thinking of leaving Nebraska the sky splits open. Flat brown dirt turns to soupy mud. Your shoes sink and stick. You fall to your knees. Nebraska says, "Is this really what you want?" Nebraska says, "If you leave you can't come back." You listen carefully for some hint of grief, but Nebraska is matter-of-fact. You are packing your bags.

Nebraska can take it. You whisper goodbye and Nebraska is gone.

Your new home is the highway. You roll the windows down and the music up. On the interstate, food comes wrapped in plastic. You must eat with one hand, one hand on the wheel. Sometimes at night you miss Nebraska. You scrunch your pillow into a giant mouth and kiss it, saying, "Oh darling Nebraska, you big hairy bison," and other things you are ashamed to repeat in daylight. Your friends tell you not to be silly. "There are lots of cute states. Try something with hills." But you remember oceans of razor-sharp grasses. Long, flat stretches of nothing but brown. You remember the slur of stones beneath bare feet as you searched the riverbed for fossils. You remember the harvest moon staining your skin blood red.

Every morning you walk past the house with broken windows and break another window. The shiny Valentine inside scrubs dishes at the sink. Think hard enough about broken glass and it becomes rain in a tumbleweed town, drowning out the neighbors' quarrels. You've had to invent this life to make it work. Try speaking but no sound comes out, try tenderness but it twists in an instant. Think blood on the mattress. Try running, and not for the scenery.

Don't think I've forgotten. I haven't forgotten anything to do with you. Not the stairs leading down into the sauna; not the sauna's broken knob; not you undressing; not you drenched; not you alone at the foot of the stairs, the clothes in your arms some damp thing dying. You're climbing the stairs, slick from the sauna. If the corpse starts talking, who will it tell? At the top of the stairs, the narrow landing, and then the living room. You're in the living room. You're in the living room, and I'm just no good. You hold the needle over the record, a song from childhood. We would not have been friends. At the center of the room you drop the dead thing. When I touch your zipper the diamond needle goes down.

Your mother's maiden name was Dexler. My mother's maiden name was Dexter, and we remarked on this coincidence, our secret handshake. It felt breezy, sharing *Dex* with you. Secretly we each liked our ending better—your *-ler*, with its drunken waltzing; my *-ter*, with its sequined tap dancing. I met your mother twice. The first time was an accident. I was holding your place in line while you went back for something you'd forgotten. A woman stood behind me; I helped her unload her basket. Then I heard your boots and turned around. I asked for her name. *Gladys,* she said. I introduced you to your mother at Madison Market. Later I saw what the resemblance was: the way you shook hands like strangers to love.

You were the only woman in a workplace of men. Every morning you put on a dress and drove off. When you left the house you wore your ring on a chain, but at night you came home with a married girl's finger. On the walls of your cubicle: photos of your brother so you wouldn't have to tell all those men about me.

Something to do with airplanes: I think you were responsible for making sure they could fly. You had a list of parts tattooed on your arm and checked off items with erasable ink. Over the roof pilots wrote the real story: how to move war from one site to the next. Production hangars had clouds on the ceiling. You'd fly in one plane to check out the next. The way to test propellers against damage due to flying birds was to shoot frozen chickens out of a cannon. You warned me not to phone you at work. The police called us *roommates* when they wrote the report.

As a child I dismantled baked goods to see how they worked. A little sugar and history repeats itself *merrily merrily merrily merrily* like the boat I thought I'd grow up to be. Big boat, big merrily. *Be still inside yourself. Be stealth.* Nervous arrangements of words played house. Red ribbons in my hair like an ornery horse. I went barefoot, pretending I was at the beach. When someone used bleach it stayed in the washer. Laundry detergent smelled like birthday cake flowers. Damp clothes spelled *HELP* on the linoleum floor.

It starts with a squirrel, but the squirrel isn't in the same state of being from beginning to ending. You're watching me from your window. I'm walking the perimeter of your house, shoes clicking on gravel, when I see the cage. I knew you had guns because you made me touch them. I knew you shot them once a month with your friends. When we were alone—oh, everyone knows that story. The story of what I found in the cage. It wasn't a bird. It was the squirrel you were bothered by. He was always running from the telephone wire to the tree beside your bedroom window to the wire again, clattering. It was a noisy game. I named him Nelson and dropped peanuts when you weren't looking. One night when you were drinking you took out a gun and put it on the floor. I got nervous, asked you to put it away. *No,* you said, *guns don't just go off.* It sounded like a bumper sticker. The gun lay on the floor between us and I knew what you were thinking. I could see what you were thinking. *I hate men,* you said.

We lay in the tall grass. We were just girls then. This was all written in the palm of your hand.

We woke up one morning and the sign sat squat on your neighbor's immaculate lawn: *For Sale,* and the name of their realtor, Dean. Twin white rocking chairs paused on the porch. The night before you were screaming at me and throwing stuff. I don't remember what stuff but it broke. When we woke up their house was for sale and you said *Good* and I said nothing because I deserved it, really, the sign on my chest.

Before the four-foot rule and after midnight somebody mistakes me for one of the girls. This is why you brought me here. Mistakes are what we make together. My thighs stick to vinyl as I whisper a name I've made up on the spot. There's a room backstage where deals go down, there's room onstage for another Sabrina. I'll do what you tell me. Just tell me this isn't my grave I'm digging, tell me the speakers aren't playing our song. Over and over we scrub the dishes, over and over we dry the clothes. We break the dishes, we drop the clothes in waist-high grass by the barn out back. Red planks sink, swaying to kneeling. Swans swallow lead shot instead of gray stones.

Caution tape for breakfast, a little sadness for company: your car looks small in the hubcap of the semi beside us. If someone erased us, there'd be room in traffic for one more car. We're driving the skeletal freeway, hypodermics freckling the beach below the boxcars, city folded into a thousand cranes. *We're near, we're dear, get used to it.* I've never been good at keeping secrets. Say hello, newsprint. *Newsprint, hello.* Stars pretend to be oil on water while the oil refinery pretends to be stars. *Calling all cars. Calling all cars.* I sleep on the floor; I sleep on the table. Pale crescent worm drags the moon from its bottle. *Surrender* to the weather you became in my town. I want to lure you down the crumbly slope to the gully to the river-baby to the river-tether. Over the log-jam. Beyond us, the sea—

Someone told you it would all get easier; don't believe her. Believe in the sidewalk, cracks overgrown with weeds; believe in the neighbor's gate, swinging wide to send the dog running. Believe in paper or plastic, cars the size of houses, dealers with kerchiefs and one cuff rolled. Throw a sheet over the dead refrigerator, junked for parts, scrap metal hearts. Listen for crossfire through crosshaired trees.

At the grocery you pick a basket because it's blue. You fill it with apples because they're red. And everyone around you loves fluorescent lights, lushly orchestrated Top Forty hits, yellow signs that say *Slippery When Wet*. Supermarkets aren't dangerous; back alleys are dangerous. This is just the cereal aisle. Black holes careen toward you, one more excuse to let the lawn go. You don't repeat history to get it right. You do it to suffer, climbing the same stairs over and over, covering your windows with newsprint and foil. No one knows where you go at night—tightropes and ditches, one-way streets and floating bridges. Your hand is your hand is your hand in a fist. Press what limps to your chest and love it. Don't listen to whispers, those four-letter words. Of all the girls you grew up with, claimed, only your surname remains the same.

two

Dodge and Burn

We watched the girl through her open window. 45th Street was hot but she was on fire. We were thinking we should fuck her as she undressed in front of a face or a mirror. I said look at her hair, soft. You said look at her lips, bloom. We'd prepared our room: dog in her cage, silk over skylights because of the heat. You said she's sweet. I said three's sweeter. And after we'd take notes on who was better. Seattle had never been hotter. You had a bottle and I had a bottle. A building caught fire, rows of condos attached at the hip. Fire trucks slipped on glossy pavement. Water filled the moonlit basement. A man flew from a balcony into the air. Ash stained our hair and the whorls of our dresses. Water caressed us, the thick blue knife slicing away burnt boards and glass. We lit cigarettes off the burning grass and breathed smoke until the streets were clean, the dog lay dreaming, and you were mine again. Breezes fanned the trees and the tinderbox lawn. Both the window and the girl were gone.

These days you can't get a lap dance in Seattle because the girls are gone. Heels clutter gutters over vegetable vendors. Leopard-print shawls stutter bicycle spokes. Silver thongs poke from window-box posies. The girls are swimming. See their bright hair. Sleeves billow, angels, as they trouble the water. They float down Green River to the lip of the bay. One day the police find a girl in boxes among the clothes in someone's closet. She was drained of fluid. She was labeled and stacked. He was the one, so it seems safe to walk after dark. You hear wind whistling as winter recedes; you hear tulips pushing up from the earth; you hear the voice of the girl in the box, the voice everyone else mistakes for spring.

It was for the time in the car with him. He'd call and you'd say yes, although you'd come round to say no to the others. You'd write it down on the calendar above the sink and wash your hair the night before. He always said that he was grateful. He paid you more than the going rate. For over a year you rode in the car with him every Saturday, twenty minutes each way, forty minutes a week. You continued to take money from him after it happened. He continued to say that he was grateful. Because of these things you came to believe that what was happening was happening to a different girl.

Your next-door neighbor was always crying. Handkerchiefs froze on the line in winter, stiff white sheets of embroidered paper. The stain on your ceiling widened from an anvil into Vancouver Island. One afternoon she stood in the grass cutting her hair, which vanished as it fell into the thick of green things. *In case you're wondering, I have a web cam. People pay me to have sex and then cry.* Nights, you played chess on an upside-down milk crate, huddled together just shy of the lens. She brewed herbal tea with leaves from her garden, mint so sharp it cut teacups to shards.

You're at the corner of Commercial and Champion when the call comes in and you turn on the siren. Now you're in a room with two women. You pat down their nightgowns, examine their teeth. One has bruises, one wears a necklace. How are you going to tell them apart? Try explaining a nightmare. Try explaining a bad day at the office. Try explaining a dirty fuck. Somebody's telling the truth in your city. When her body hits bottom, the river zips up.

Blacksmith in love hoists the 9-lb hammer, forges a coffin the size of her fist. When it cools, she sets two mice inside: bodies entwined, bones dried. She seals the box with barbed wire locks, a gift for her lover as he weeps for his sister: the Green River Killer's next-to-last murder. Picking me up from the airport last August you drove the shortcut down Sea-Tac strip. Dozens of girls by the side of the road, bridges and brides in overgrown green. *Remember the river and the names in the river.* You drove for miles while I begged you to stop. That night a noise woke us, coyote or shot. We stumbled through grass, saplings sprouting where we'd gorged on cherries. When the stranger ran past us the sheet slipped her shoulders until she ran naked down Marginal Way. This was not a dream of the river but waking life: the bloodstained mouth, a scattering of seeds, saplings crowding each other to breathe.

Freeways run through fiberglass skin. A girl cuts roses into her arms. Under the West Seattle Bridge, in bustiers and bicycle shorts, the Dead Baby Bikers race the 5:19. The man beside me emails his husband: *light rain heavy traffic past the Montlake Cut.* Tabby cat curls under a monster truck, mini-monster preening in the mirrored wheels. In the vegetable garden, cracked eggs release snakes. An umbrella marries spokes from a hybrid bike, city lights a tossed bouquet for night to catch: star asters. There's a fine line between lap dancing and washing the dishes. You're smoking now that everyone's quit, ash as snow while you show me how to take it slow, not break one dish.

In another incarnation you're sitting on a dock, dangling your legs over the edge. You're new, and in this chapter I'm new, too. We're pulling splinters from our thighs, whittling pears into peaches. One of us has a dreadful disease and her hair has fallen out. But I don't know which one. In this chapter your skirt is covered with candy apples. It's shirred at the waist, fluted to your ankles. In this chapter I lift your skirt until you're blind. Beneath your skirt you wear sequined hot pants. Then you multiply and it's 1949. Fifteen dancers, their skirts a great flower, seen from above, legs unfurling in sync. And in private, what's left of privacy, in candlelight, what's left of it, legs fan, flutter, fold shut. You're less than, more than. You're a lens. My great love affair, delirious beauty, fantasy fuck-with-it of it all. Your terrible range, terrible rages. Your bee-sting pout, powdered prances. The Rockette of it all! Some girls are not girls (sashay). And in public what to say to the one who's obviously packing? Onstage, reading snippets from *The Book of Believe Me?* God in the form of great love for Rockettes. And where has the dock got to, in this story? Where is the disease, the sequined pants? What beginning, middle, end? Without order, chaos; chaos, blossom. Whittling a thigh into a tongue. Me and the remaining Rockettes onstage, preparing a funeral for the sequined city. How lovely, Lovely. My bee-sting allergy. You're in the shape of a young boy today. Toggle your screen and you're a girl

•

again. How a mouse can make anything into a cat. How a cat becomes a boy; a boy, religion. My lover in the shape of a fairy-tale ending. My fear of bee-stings, how little time it takes for me to swell—

Dangerous Cargo No Open Flames. You lit a cigarette and exhaled a dress in my direction. I undid that dress, zippers and bows. You did your little pony dance. We fought scurvy and mermaids and sirens and loons. Behind us a church rose out of green hills. Easter hymns filled the space between us. I took in God's gaze like wood ash glaze on teacups in trees. Fell to my knees. (My knees are where *gasp* goes, and *please.*) I took in girls with hathead hair, little Bibles everywhere, psalms for oats in horses' tails. Cow puppies tongued clover in fields of feathers. Ruby red apples turned lady killers: pesticide shrouds spun by seasonal pickers. Wrens sang sermons in stained glass eaves. Shock of *He is risen,* shock of the unspoken. Last year's eggs waited for unlucky children.

Two men and a dog dead on the tracks, done in by a fast train footfalls from here. Still it's here you sit, slicing avocados with your sharpened thumb. Why must we always picnic in perilous places? We're the same girl on different pages. I was you once; someday you'll be me: surrounded by cats, eating grief from a tin. Today you're lovely, your hair a hat, dowdy as God. You'd stop the train if you were walking toward the V that never ends; instead you're licking bread from butter, brewing lettuce for female troubles. Do you listen for whistles or just the facts? We're crossing tracks, leaving crumbs for rats, scratching the surface of unsuspecting brunettes. With our rowdy skirts and shared caboose the Burlington Northern can't catch us here: Rainier on one side, Puget Sound on the other.

New lovers leave the house for the first time. They follow water because following water is what they have been doing. They are learning sea, sun, sky instead of each other's features. In secret each fears the other's mouth will fade. But look at the houses! Flower boxes, flamingos, flags! Holding hands, they step across asphalt into the new world where all will know.

three

Echolocation

After we'd made animals of each other I asked for her name. This bought us time, brought us to a room unlike this one. Why the stage set of a bedroom instead of a cage? I hadn't meant to bruise her arm but grasped—the bay beyond us red, stunned flat—with a grip that seemed at first a suture. I reached for her in the language of understanding—wanting to, I mean—not knowing skin wasn't the place to enter. The juxtaposition of one world against another meant someone had to make a choice, lean into syntax and break it. She worried about me. I paid her for this. She moved faster in stillness than I moved in speed.

Interruptions are autographs, names too small to decipher. In heels, in harness she sits on her hands. She won't make a sound until she knows I'm watching. Subsidized newscasts distort the burning. The cities are perfect in her dirty world. She stares out the window at a brown dog and sometimes a white one. At intermission she listens for rain through a skylight pointed in the wrong direction. I let her watch and then I watch her. She unbuttons me and I unzip her. I pace with a book on my head. Her house faces Prospect but the address is Elm.

She sets blue flowers in a vase of blue water, stems sticking up, blossoms face down. She drowns conversation in touch, a language others have to pay her for. Haven't I been here before, panties in my back pocket a backhanded compliment? There was a door but I didn't use it. There was a chance for neglect or escape. I drape her solitude in dreamless sleep. We're wearing matching music today and isn't this lovely, sex without a lens or a man? How we light each other's dresses. How she dresses and undresses. How quiet the world before the word *belief*. I release doves from the crook of her crooked smile. She leads small ruined lives into the midst of this.

I shoved her I did and sheets for the story I couldn't write fluttered over us, catching our throats as motes. She deserved it, fingering someone else's hair into castles. All that blue and purple in the language we'd borrowed. Before the shove came this noise, a tractor rumbling lug nuts down the country road we'd colonized or Boeing testing another warplane. Noise was my machine, my bad heart timing out, alarm going off to wake up what was weeping. We were ex-gays not yet ex or exes who'd made a mess of things. I wrestled the phone from its cradle, crooking my arm and freeing the cord. A restraining order that meant No Texas. My side, swipe, hip, hype—shove. Because I could. Because she still cared what my thighs did. Because of my place among her exes: white as weddings, suburbs, harm.

She slipped the ring off her finger. Dropped it on the dresser in the bowl I made: a terrible mistake in clay, afraid as I was of earth, of spinning, of the mad mad wheel. We might've spoken of murder. We might've spoken, but the quiet bled like light, was light, was night resisted inch by inch, as a good girl takes a dress to wife. She used a knife to cut away stern plaster. After, she made me very still, stiff blush heat of an oven door deciding whether or not to temperature. She made me a statue, stone bust welded to one museum's steel wall. My fall was hers, catch clasp latch after. We might've spoken of rapture: rain running Railroad Avenue, train whistling at skirts on the line. Her nakedness was mine, blind wingless angel, listening to junkies trading kisses for wine.

·

Litany, refrain, schoolhouse tile scraped thin by chairs pushed back in Disaster Class. Those lessons I skipped? I want them back. In dreams I take tests in nothing but sneaks, naked thighs sticking to a lefty desk. Lunch box, lined paper, the doll of me sits there, blackening circles with a steady hand.

Freed from the constraint of narrative you wait on a bus that never arrives. You like it, like you like your likeness on the head of a coin worth less than one cent. Dictionary of you, website of you, indie film festival of you undressing. For someone else. In a burning building. You're riding a mechanical bull. I mean—you're beautiful. You're hanging out at the Hotel Helena. I mean—in hell. Polar bears are already there, waiting for floes that won't float over. Kindergarten casts them as sugary fiction and whose fault is it that the ice caps are melting? You're using your fists to solve everyday problems. I mean—your breasts to suggest sexual tension. You're out of control. I mean—out of paper. Bleak bodice ripper. I mean—you're in love.

Swirled tight, trussed, manic, most trusted. You love hills, swells, waves of sand, waves of water. You love traffic on bridges that might split in two. You love stairs leading to stairs leading to stairs leading to ice cream stands. Shards of pottery as good as a map. You love fractured control towers and the very broken Alaskan Way Viaduct. You love squat corner stores and barber-pole stop signs. You love the idea of privacy in a city of windows, the idea of light in a city of shadows.

Into the realm of the not night Math Boi enters with his knock knees. What was nuclear becomes disaster. The awful taxonomy of sex slurs its pinks to the pales of Pompeii. Math Boi turns cartwheels, her skirt over her head in an obscure cheer. Math Boi does business with friends and the French, his camera flirting, shutter fluttering, capturing the core of the everyday.

(or so they say)

Math Boi blows on a dandelion's fur until it turns to fire. She presses her cheek to the eucalyptus.

(that is, until everything changes)

Sad little Math Boi. Sad and lost his sparkles. If she wrote in journals she would have pages about a belt missing its buckle. All almond is gone from the world, and all thyme, and the only taste left is raisin, which he doesn't like. She woke smelling scents she hadn't smelled for months and knew the Belovéd was crossing over to some other country. If there's a map to letting go of someone you love so much you're on fire Math Boi is not the cartographer. A little egg against the bowl, a whisk, and a new cake is supposed to appear on the table, full of candles and guests' open mouths.

(Everyone else has bad clothes and bad hair and will, in time, be revealed to be wearing bad underwear from a store in the mall.)

Math Boi is little, humped over with the weight of losing, but there are doors everywhere if he cares to knock. Little star, little firebird, big boots, vanilla. Surely loss can be made into something beautiful: a sudden suitcase, a train wreck narrowly avoided, a whistle from the lips of her lover on the cusp of a spiral stair.

My love and I made a baby from tangles in our hair; from roots, beads, and ginger beer; from the long tongue of memory. She was neither flesh of our flesh, nor craft, but a crashing cross between. The sheen of her skin silked without milk. The rise and fall of her chest felt best under my coat. Her throat wore necklaces I bought for my love; her fingers, gloves my love bought for me. She was the perfect baby for women so busy we sometimes forgot to put on our shoes. She cared for us, no matter what essence might cause our friends to quietly forget us. She slept under the sill in a hanging basket, flew to the attic in search of ghosts. An accident of pleasure—we'd been trying for months—her tenderness saved us, until the day someone told us she wasn't real

A man stands on the corner of Prospect and Holly flapping his wings as if to fly. If you watch long enough the dead return with beautiful wings, sweep down to street level, glide through a window, and sit at your table. The dead return— they do. Only open a window and there it is, light finally reaching you after all this time. At the end each gesture carried meaning: the cool cloth, my hands light on his feet. My father had a brisk way about him. As a child, the gardener let him hide from cruelty in great beds of lavender. My father wore velvet trousers and carried a trumpet in a leather case. My hands pressed the cloth to his feet, nested with robin's egg veins. My fallen starling. *Darling.* In death he flew as ash, something for wind to be concerned about. For me to carry in a plastic bag. If flying were meant for us, how would we find it? The corner of Prospect and Holly is empty, save for the people tall buildings become.

four

Empty Girl, Pink Sleeve

It sometimes happened that the wife liked you, too, and the two of them approached you. Or rather, the wife approached you, initially as if alone, and then unfolded the invitation. You could always tell when it was a package deal. The wife wore a particular type of ring and sat in a particular type of way. And a particular type of honesty distinguished this approach from double-crossing, which was another art altogether, more difficult to spot. It happened again last month. A woman you knew from Adult Beginning Ballet invited you out to lunch. In the dressing room this woman often mentioned her husband, so there was no question, you thought, of a misunderstanding. Not that this woman sent signals other than suburban: the diet, the book club, the mini-van. You could tell that the husband had given the okay for her to have fun with one of the girls. What you hadn't expected was the word *love*. You slept with women who slept with women who did not have husbands. You were not concerned with engagement rings, birth control, taking his name. So when you agreed to lunch and found yourself at a chain restaurant eating overcooked pasta, you were not prepared for the heavy word *love*. You tried to act flattered and set the woman at ease, but you always said no with a husband involved.

Everyone in your circle had slept together at least once. At the center was a talented artist, a man who wore kilts and only fucked girls. You fucked girls and boys, but mostly girls. Most of the girls fucked boys, but fucked girls occasionally, mostly you. Most of the boys fucked girls, but drunk on absinthe they'd forget the rules. There was another girl like you who fucked mostly girls, but you had a fight and she moved away. Dating outside the circle was thought to be a necessary evil. It introduced new blood to old ties. It challenged your set to stay tough, to stay lean. Rarely did anyone from outside make it inside, but even I could tell when someone wanted in. I never wanted in. I watched from a distance. But I wanted you, and you were inside.

———————•———————

You knew the back alley to every address. You knew the shallows and the buried glass. You knew how many inches the Viaduct shifted when an earthquake shook the ground beneath it. You knew Seattle like you ran Seattle and some people said you were part of a gang. Your friends slept with shotguns and listened for sirens. You walked like you knew where the bodies were buried.

The smoking tent outside The Anvil was swollen. Someone set a chair on fire and someone else put it out with his coat. Smoke clouded your throat, scarf too dark to see the scar there, threadbare. You walked into The Anvil and I followed behind. You wore Faux Cherry Red lipstick—my color, too. A barbed wire heart on a twisted chain. You wanted the bartender to know my name. You wanted me to be safe in The Anvil if something happened. *I'm giving her the tour,* you said. You pointed out the bathroom—the room behind us that said *Bathroom*—and said you'd be back in five minutes, tops. I looked down at my soda. One of the seeds from the lemon had fallen to the bottom of the glass. The soda had two straws, pink and yellow, because it was diet. You always assumed I was watching my weight. I kicked my feet against the counter. You were bending over a pretty girl at a table full of pretty girls. I tried to give a peanut to the black Lab padding around the bar because dogs love me. This dog did not love me. A man had his arm around the back of your chair, playing with your hair as if he knew you or wanted to. I rummaged a newspaper out of recycling. Someone asked if you were in the basement but there was no basement. *I mean the roof.* A guy stumbled into me. *Are you Swedish?* he asked. *You have a huge face, like Swedish people.*

Sex with you meant Scandinavian pop. There was something of the fjord about you, chilly state issue of the gleam in your eyes. From the living room, eerie high-pitched wailing: something about sky as a method of transport, confusing *stars* with *carpool lane*. You promised me pain always led to pleasure. Took an orange from the copper-topped table and killed it, peeling skin from bone. You set in stone the shape you wanted me to ink in skin: arabesque, ruffled hem of a lifted dress. You slit the novel I wore as a skirt. Read the end first. Built stairs out of matchsticks to your low-ceilinged attic where we listened to planes shaking under the sky. We shared sheet metal sheets, blowtorches for candles, fiber-glass lingerie in a heap on the floor. My wolf, your door. Our h-ever after. This is the story of torching the rafters, blazes as bridges between faith and decay. Come nightfall the stairs folded into umbrellas. What covered our faces was always homemade.

Perhaps it seems odd that your dog's name and my older brother's name were the same. Perhaps it seems odd that both of them died tragically, mysteriously, and that we kept what we could to remember them by. Perhaps it seems odd that you preserved a snowball on a table in your well-heated home.

I may be a liar, but it's my version of this story you'll remember.

Waking, we noticed a man at our window. Thud on the porch came a chair through the door. His long sleeves caught fire, bloodride verticals, orange jutting into blue. After, ash. We cleared a plot out back, clematis clinging to a silver cross above the loam where we scattered stones, where we spooked each other threatening treason. *I can keep a secret* in unison, hand to breast like school. Our words cooled the scar where he stood in bright sleeves while we watched through the window, our bedroom window, first as he watched us, then as he burned. At first we were concerned someone might miss him. But the knock on the door by our window was wind. We had nothing to do with its tangles: beets, tomatoes, basil, saplings choking old trees. Under the eaves wind tousled sheets on the bed where we'd stared at the man staring down. It seems impossible now, some seventh circle of hell. Words breaking glass. Bright hands reaching. The match.

You shot me by the rails, three men watching from a tent under the bridge. I stood in broken glass, hair escaping my barrette: some kind of saint already, smack on the tracks with headlights for company.

There has to be an ending, but you don't stop. We're driving toward train tracks under the West Seattle Bridge. We're driving toward the dangerous part, the place where the train comes fast without warning. Listen for the whistle. The whistle. Where. The train speeds forward as the best trains do and you drive your truck like the devil I wished for. This is the moment we've been waiting for, Darling. You call me *Babe* and ruffle my hair. The red light sweats and uncrooks its elbows. The red light lowers its candy cane arms. The red light reads the long line on your palm as you keep on driving, toward headlights, toward home.

Planes overhead hang where you left them, stars against a bent steel sky. This isn't love, but it might be mercy: talking to myself as if the streets might forgive me, fool me into thinking red lights go green. *Come in, sit down, would you like a drink, a bed with clean sheets, a hand over your mouth?* Bad news travels fast in a seaside town. There's glass where a fist punched through a window; there's blood on the window. The fist is mine. The story is ours, and we know it ends badly. The abandoned house bleeds radio all night long. Happiness is hard to describe: birds seen from below, sky seen from above. The small mad heart at the center of things stalls mid-tick.

Welcome to the Shatterloft, room of ruins. I've known motion but never this gesturing toward loss: flame-haired toddler in a pink dress, left sleeve empty, flag without a country, anthem calling me thirty years ahead. In bed you dream with both hands. Drown deep. Cheat sleep. Sheep castration bands bind your hook. Cradle me in the crook of your never-was-an-elbow-there. You roll cigarettes with one wrist, pink tongue to silk, ash after smoke. What broke against the bowl of our bodies was my crowded mouth. Now tell me, Empty, how will I love a new lover's whole-ness, her two useless hands?

Bills in the mail, streets lined with trees surviving another day of car exhaust, another day of reckless driving. Tear the hem of my dress so it falls above my knees. Now it's spring, dumb faith in rebirth, rabbits multiplying under the neighbor's junked cars, gold light climbing as winter recedes, everyone missing a language, a limb. I used to fall in love so easily, bedroom bright with broken glass. Start over: an envelope with nothing in it, freckled bird in a tethered tree.

We broke into an abandoned factory full of rusty box-cars, set fire to gasoline rags in bottles. High noon found us waltzing to ghost town music: an ice cream truck turned prairie nursery, coyote pups asleep on the seat. We spilled into the street. I stilled you by the waist, pushed you up against the red of someone's car. My nerve that afternoon, not even pretending I was looking for change or changing my shoes. Shaking your skirt like cloth over a table. The perfect detail of your hair on the hood. Cars veering, people drifting, the opening opening. Your hem the day's headline. Not thinking of war. You told me the story of Jesse Garon Presley, stillborn twin brother to Elvis the King. We listened to Johnny Cash, drank beer from bottles you kept in the bath. Sleep with me again under the high-silled window, silver with raindrops—no, barbed wire. Take cover. Something beautiful gleams through the fault line. The diamonds are glass. We shine like they're real.

Carol Guess is the author of two novels, *Seeing Dell* (Cleis Press, 1996) and *Switch* (Calyx Books, 1998); a memoir, *Gaslight* (Odd Girls Press, 2001), and a collection of poetry, *Femme's Dictionary* (Calyx Books, 2004). Forthcoming titles include a poetry collection, *Love Is A Map I Must Not Set On Fire* (VRZHU Press) and a novel, *Homeschooling* (PS Publishing). She is an associate professor of English at Western Washington University, and lives on the Washington coast with her spouse, writer Elizabeth Colen.

A Note About the Type

The interior of this book is set in the typeface Dante. Originally designed for letterpress printing in the mid-1950s, Dante was the result of a six-year collaboration between Giovanni Mardersteig, a printer, book designer, and typeface artist, and Charles Malin, one of the great punch-cutters of the twentieth century. The two worked closely together to ensure the typeface was easy to read, designing the lowercase characters with a subtle horizontal stress that eases the strain on the eye as it moves across the page. The typeface was named after Boccaccio's *Trattatello in laude di Dante*, which, in 1955, was the first publication to use the new face.

In the late 1950s, Monotype convinced Mardersteig to allow the company to develop a machine-set version of Dante. With the help of 20-year-old Matthew Carter, they also persuaded him to develop additional weights beyond the roman and italics Mardersteig originally created for letterpress. An immediate success, Dante was quickly released for phototypesetting and then in the 1990s was reworked by Monotype's Ron Carpenter for digital use.

—*Melissa Gruntkosky*